T0209078

Prayer *and* Forgiveness

Prayer *and* Forgiveness

COUNSEL AND GUIDANCE ON SPIRITUAL GROWTH

Melina Christensen

ARCHWAY PUBLISHING

Archway Publishing books may be ordered
through booksellers or by contacting:

Archway Publishing
1663 Liberty Drive
Bloomington, IN 47403
www.archwaypublishing.com
844-669-3957

ISBN: 978-1-6657-0138-9 (sc)
ISBN: 978-1-6657-0139-6 (e)

Library of Congress Control Number: 2021900351

Print information available on the last page.

Archway Publishing rev. date: 04/12/2021

Preface

I am sitting by the fireside, reading the final proofs of this translation of Melina Christensen's book *Prayer and Forgiveness*. Outside, dawn has come. It is autumn, and the day already has a promising look to it. It didn't when I first started reading Melina's book. It was 2014, and I had suffered a nervous breakdown. As I lay in our spare bedroom, trying to figure out who I was and how I had ended up there on the couch, I found her book on the shelf. It stood there, waiting for me. I had bought it because it had the image of a water lily on the cover, and we had used that for our wedding invitations, way back when. And then I liked the prayer bit in the title. Forgiveness was not on my chart, least of all for myself, but I started reading anyway. What other options did I have?

As I read and did the techniques of praying for forgiveness, my outlook changed. Today, that is seven years back, and my life has changed. That change came early, and as a wish to give something back, I started translating the book into English. In this process, I looked up its author and got some backstory on the volume. Melina had sat down each evening over one summer, by candlelight, after the kids were asleep and channeled the book. OK. See, I don't know much about that. I was brought up in a scientific way. My take is that most people could write an eight-hundred-pager like Thomas Mann's *Buddenbrooks*, if they wanted to badly enough, but that real mastery lies in giving his slender 120-page *Death in Venice* its shape and impact. That's my measure. Melina had no former training as a writer. No bestseller in her writers´ belt. As I read *Prayer and Forgiveness*, I was reminded about this. There are no sidetracks. No detours. No chitchat. As I reread the translation, I still detect no fat on its frame. That's high measure. You need years and years to go there. So I guess she did channel it after all.

One thing that struck me, though, seven years ago, was the admonishing words and solemn tone of the White Brotherhood—a group of supposedly elevated souls who formed a council for the benefit of humankind on the next level. In 2014, we had just ridden out the 2009 financial crash, Obama was president, and the Paris Charter was underway. Things looked bright. Today, I see their point in bringing "hope and wisdom before the great challenge that humans will face." We have the COVID-19 pandemic, racial unrest, economic recession, and division between ideologies and religious beliefs, both at home and abroad. The publication of this sleek volume on spiritual guidance and counsel could not be more timely or accurate. It is my hope that others will benefit from this, as I have done myself.

—Morten Meldgaard
Langebåt, Norway
October 2020

Introduction

_____

To all of humanity from the White Brotherhood:

Through this channel, which has now been opened to us, we will try to contact you, to bring hope and wisdom before the great challenge that humans will face.

You will be tested, as it is of great importance that each of you stand fast and hold your own ground, rooted in your inner truth, the divine truth.

It is a cardinal point, as it takes great courage and strength to bring the divine light down on earth in much bigger quantum than you have been used to doing.

Every soul must search itself before it undertakes the task of becoming a bearer of the divine light.

Everyone carries this ability to bring forth the light, but as always, with any kind of work or spiritual development, it will take predecessors—human souls who are already qualified to work with and for the light.

It is a prerequisite for this work that anyone planning to undertake it has first cleansed himself or herself. We will help you achieve this end; all you need to do is to pray for this purification.

The next step will be that you have the courage to look

truly and fully into your own eyes, to accept whatever comes to the surface from the depths of your soul, and to ask for forgiveness so that all shadow can be redeemed.

Forgiveness is a key word in this because when you ask for forgiveness, you practice humbleness, and humbleness enables you to know where all strength and power reside.

Any human being must, in due course, go into this soul-searching and work honestly and without ulterior motive so that he or she is able to stand forth as a beautiful and authentic example of the divine love and creative power.

The opening for searching of each individual soul is latent with many human beings, and those who truly want to bring forth light in the human realm will be given all the spiritual help they need.

They only need to ask for it.

1

The Challenge

Never before have we and our guardian angels been closer to humans than at the present time.

Now is the time for the challenge—light will have its way. The light wants to transform human emotions of sorrow and despair, which is also why these emotions seem to flourish at the present time.

There is an exchange between light and dark, almost like an inhale and exhale of breath, between the light of the spirit and the darkness of human emotion. The more the pressure of light descends on earth, the further darkness and desperation will surface in the human realm.

You will experience that earth and your life-world will seem more desperate, more intangible. All this is only to allow the helpers and light-bearers to receive the light in order to transform the feelings of sorrow, despair, hate, enmity, and debasement that you have created for yourself.

All these emotions arise from your fear of each other and of life, in general.

You have forgotten why you are here, and you have

chosen, instead, to fight one another. For what? Honor? Or the shame of bringing grief and destruction in others' lives?

Go deep into yourself. Contact your innermost being, the voice in you, through which you are connected to the divine truth.

Ask for help to be made conscious in order to rise above the fights you are fighting and the conflicts you have chosen.

More often than not, you are fighting a good cause, but you forget that each and every human being is responsible for his or her actions.

Collective responsibility will not help the individual when it is time to make accounts. Then everybody will have to answer for his or her own actions, and the collective aspect of the good cause will have gone.

Do not succumb to bad consciousness or feelings of guilt. These emotions will not help anyone, least of all you. Instead, you must pray for forgiveness for yourself and others, and then work on changing your behavior.

When everyone, each on their own, goes into themselves and seeks the wisdom of their hearts, a great love of humankind will arise, regardless of race, status, or past conflict.

In this, everybody is equal, and no one is closer or farther removed from the love of God.

God loves and forgives everyone, but at the same time, the divine wish is that everyone will forgive everyone else—a wish that humanity will learn to use forgiveness as a way of purifying and cleansing itself.

In order to use forgiveness in this way, each and every

one must learn to understand themselves and then their fellow humans.

They need to learn to see themselves and who they are and to understand the background for their actions in this life and time.

This work starts with the individual, where everyone studies themselves introspectively—their actions, their motives, their intent.

The moment you send out something impure or unfriendly, be it in thought, action, or word, a path is also created for its return. This is one of the primary spiritual and karmic laws.

When you give out unkind thoughts and emotions, you create an opening for the same unkindness to meet you at a future date.

When you acknowledge this, a part of your work will be to accept the unkind thoughts and emotion you have sent out in your previous life and to ask for forgiveness for each individual thought and emotion.

This will demand a thorough uncovering of your patterns of thought and your emotional life. Then, you will have to disentangle yourself in order to clarify your motives and intentions.

Everyone must come to an understanding of their previous actions in any given situation, not to judge themselves or their actions but to look at their past with love and a clarity of mind.

This is the challenge: do not to judge yourself or succumb to bad consciousness. Too often, you judge yourself so that you lose the spark of life, creativity, and decisiveness.

You lose your natural connection with the divine truth because you make yourself feel unworthy.

No other single thought is more destructive than this.

Every human being is made in the image of God, and by loving and caring for yourself, you can grow and become part of divine truth again.

Every human being carries the spark within himself or herself—the sacred flame of the heart—and by feeding this flame, you will increase your contact to your higher self and, eventually, to your contact with the spiritual world.

The divine truth is laid down in the heart of any human being. It is time that more human beings realize this truth and commence the work of light, exactly where they are placed, in the present of this life-world, the realm of earth.

Working Sentences for "The Challenge"

- The challenge will stand between the light of the spirit and the darkened emotions of the human realm.
- Light wants to descend and transform these emotions.
- Ask for help to make yourself conscious.
- Work on understanding yourself; then pray for forgiveness in order to cleanse yourself and near yourself to your inner core—your true nature.
- Everything you give out will return to you.

- Use your intellect to uncover your emotional life and patterns of thought.
- Separate yourself from others by the power of forgiveness.
- Do not judge yourself; try, instead, to understand and accept yourself in order to heighten your love of yourself.

2

Purification

———————

By cleansing yourself and becoming liberated in your spirit, you will open up the possibility of transforming the energy of dark emotions and negative powers, which at present govern certain aspects of human life.

Purification comes through forgiveness, but in order to forgive, you must first lay bare your emotions.

This is not done by suppressing them but by finding a meaningful way of releasing them—*meaningful* in the sense that all human beings enable themselves to feel and to welcome their emotions.

Like it or not, the reality of emotions is that they belong to you; they reside in you, and now is the time for you to welcome them and take them home. This is not done by pointing your emotions, such as sorrow or anger, at others but by quietly accepting that these emotions are part of you, a part that is now claiming acceptance and recognition from you.

Many therapists do great work in this field, and many people make a great effort through different activities.

What needs to be done, however, is the full realization of the process of purification, which is a stepping-stone to the ultimate goal of living in peace—not only with yourself, but with your fellow humans.

So that each human being gains a spiritual dimension in the endeavour to heal himself or herself, an authentic connection to the divine truth should be reestablished. This is often achieved through therapy or self-strengthening activities, which are then given the optimal conditions of bringing human beings into balance and harmony with their existence.

Self-development should aim at empowering human beings to consider and handle their emotions from a broader perspective. We also might say that human beings should mature into rising above these emotions in order to consider them from the knowledge point of their spirit selves. Emotions will not appear so dense and complicated, and the spirit will see new pathways through these emotions, by which humans develop.

When human beings give acceptance to themselves and understand how the inner life is formed, they will stop judging themselves. This will enable them to go to the next step, a new experience of inner peace. Through this experience of peace within themselves, they will gain peace with their fellow humans.

Working Sentences for "Purification"

- You must let yourself feel your emotions, take them in, and release them.
- Give *acceptance* to yourself and your emotions.
- Be conscious that when you purify yourself, you release both conscious and unconscious emotions.
- The spiritual dimension is cardinal in any self-development practice.
- Emotional release will provide peace, understanding, and acceptance of yourself and others.

3

Judgment and Prejudice

Too much is being destroyed by judgment. People meet, they size each other up, and they pass judgment from the mere appearance of their outer shells. This creates distance between human beings, based on insecurity and fear of being judged. At the same time, this makes us hide our inner beauty even more. We hide our inner lives so deeply within ourselves that we actually forget about them and lose our internal consciousness.

The outer garment of the body is merely temporal. True quality is found within.

If you really want to meet someone, then search for his or her inner values, and look deeply into the person's eyes to see if light and love are found there.

Too many romantic relationships take their point of departure from physical attraction, where outer appearance seems to have great relevance. Many people experience that the joy of love becomes hollow if it is based only on bodily contact. Loneliness of the individual increases, rather than decreases, through this type of relationship.

This happens because the individuals in a couple have been attracted by outer appearances, thus pushing the inner life to the background and hiding their true selves from each other.

It seems too dangerous to show one's own inner self when everything is judged on outer appearance. When the feeling of hollowness emerges, you start to look for reasons why.

It often is too hard and painful for you to look fully into yourself and claim responsibility for your emotions, so instead, you look to your partner and to his or hers flaws or scarcity.

In this, you most certainly are headed for the end of your relationship, unless you succumb to the situation and choose to continue living a suppressed life with a decrease in life energy.

Your partner becomes a mirror for your own suppressed inner life. When you think you are seeing his or her faults, you are, in reality, seeing your own shortcomings.

This will lead you to a state where you will blame your partner for things that are really within yourself, things that you will not recognize or tolerate within yourself. Sometimes, if the problem is of another character, you must realize that you cannot continue to live together if you truly wish to grow and develop.

In this case, you must be true to yourself, without regard to material constraints. You must rest assured that the meaning of life for each individual is to live in correspondence with his or her own inner truth.

Every prejudice creates distance, and human beings hurt each other much more than they realize by feeling that they have the right to comment on the behavior and lives of others.

Too often, we are met by prejudice, and in this, we are tested, if we are able to hold our ground and stay true to ourselves.

All human beings must work on finding their own natures and live their lives according to this. To fulfill this goal, they do not need the judgment and prejudice of others.

No human beings have the right to pass judgment on others. Judgment is a deviation of the universal principle of love and compassion that is manifested in the fact that we are all born equal.

Every human being has a justification; every being has a purpose. It is only up to God and the single human being alone to judge if that human being is living in accordance with his or her true nature and divine purpose.

Every single being has its own inner truth, a contract with God, and all human beings have a path they need to walk. It is beyond the faculties of others to judge whether or not another fellow being is living up to the clauses in that contract.

Your only guidance for actions is the spiritual law of ethical rules.

All human beings are equal. No one can judge or measure another. The task for each one is to live in harmony and take full responsibility for himself or herself.

In this way, there is no need to condemn others or find their faults, as you ought to know that what you see as wrong in others and what you base your judgment and prejudice on are actually already within yourself.

When you truly understand this, you will stop the hunt for faults and mistakes in others. You will release one another, and you will be able to concentrate on the real job at hand—namely, to take the entire world and all of its beings back into balance, while bringing the divine light down on earth by letting it shine from your heart.

Before everything else, the work that each individual must do is of cardinal importance.

The more human beings open up to this work, the faster and more powerful will be the cleansing of the human karma, and a new world—a new way of living together—will be opened up to you.

It is important right now that you take to these divine insights:

- Humanity is about to purify its collective karma.
- Energies and emotions that have been suppressed or shifted will surface in each individual and in societies at large.
- By consciously working for the release and scattering of darkness, you become the bearer of divine light.
- That any work in accordance with the spiritual world or divine plan always takes it point of departure in the single individual.

In order to be a worthy predecessor, you must always search your inner world and your inner truth, and take your action from there.

Working Sentences for "Judgment and Prejudice"

- Condemnation creates distances between human beings.
- Outer attraction creates emptiness and loneliness.
- In relationships, you will look to your partner to find the cause of loneliness.
- To do this is an attempt to escape from looking within yourself.
- Stand up for yourself. Remember that each and every one must live in concordance with his or her own inner truth
- You have no right to judge one another
- Every single human being has his or her own divine plan.
- No one but God can deem if a human being is living according to his or her own nature and the nature of this divine plan.
- Human beings must take their action from spiritual laws on ethical rules:
- All human beings are equal.
- The biggest task is to live in harmony with yourself.
- Every human being must learn to take responsibility for himself or herself and not to place responsibility or blame on others.

4

Do Not Lose Courage

In order not to lose courage, you will need a little more than a month or two to master these tasks.

It will take years for you to lift the veil that has been covering your eyes. But considering how long you have been wandering in darkness, the mere attention and wish for enlightenment will raise your spirits and lift the veil covering your consciousness a great deal.

Your energies will become lighter, and you must always remember that even though you are doing this huge work individually, you are working for the sake of all humanity.

This means that by lifting your own level of energy, you are contributing to lifting the energy level of all of humanity. This makes as good sense to you, as it does to us.

5

Words

Of greatest importance for the development of human consciousness is the realization that words become reality.

Your words do not disappear in thin air. They produce energy—energy that surrounds you and others, energy that lingers after the words have been spoken. You must realize that what you say and how you say it will show itself in the field of energy that surrounds you.

Your words hold great power; the words of everybody hold power. It is of great importance that you guard and measure your words.

Thinking before speaking is a way of the wise but even better is to feel before you speak.

Feel if what you are about to say is in alignment with your heart and sensible to the situation at hand.

What is it that you want to say?

Why do you want to say it?

To whom do you speak? What possibility does he or she hold in order to understand you, as to using your words in a constructive and nourishing manner?

Too often, you throw words at each other; you shout and harass; and you hurt each other more than you realize.

Words of anger or of hurt will stick to the person you speak to, and there, the words will create a lack of self-esteem. The words will become flesh.

Know that everything you speak will be taken seriously, even if it does not seem so in the actual situation.

Know that the person to whom you speak will remember your words, and from those words, the person will create an image of himself or herself in relation to what you have spoken.

If you feel that you have spoken unjust words, be grand enough to tell the person you have addressed. Tell him or her that you have been too harsh, and ask the one to whom you have done injustice for forgiveness.

You can do this in so many ways. You don't need to use the word *forgiveness*, but you must always go in person and say that your mind has changed and that your previous words were wrong.

Do not underestimate your words or the meaning they carry for others. Practice the control of your words when you speak.

It is indeed a hard practice, but if your wish is sincere, and you feel a deep-rooted respect for your fellow human beings, you will be given the wisdom to know when it is best to be silent.

Many things can be said, if you measure your words.

Do not ever attack others, but start from your own end of the stick.

Tell about your feelings—how you sense a given situation. Very importantly, rest in what is right for you.

Whatever the answer is, hold your own ground. Do not let yourself be persuaded, but search for the truth in your own heart. Calmly insist on your own point, and let the others share their views. Do not let this make you insecure.

This does not mean that you cannot change your mind. Changing your mind through dialogue is called human development.

But if you are certain in your heart, hold your ground.

You can always go deep inside and search for the answer because your higher self will know the truth.

Working Sentences for "Words"

- Words create energy and hold great power.
- Learn how to feel the wisdom of your heart before you speak.
- What do you want to say? And why? Is it constructive to the other party?
- Be ready to admit your mistakes.
- Practice the control of your tongue.

Never attack others with words, but start with your own experience: "I am sensing …" or "It seems to me that …."

- Hold your ground and the value of your opinion if you feel that it is right.

6

Thoughts

———————

Just like words, your thoughts also become reality.

Perhaps this is harder to grasp, as it takes place in a realm that is invisible to most human beings.

But you must realize that thoughts are energy, and that everything you send out will come back to you, just like your words.

Again, do not judge yourself. Just start anew and try to become conscious of this.

Every unkind thought you think, in reality, is pointed against you because, in reality, humanity is one.

Every single human being is part of humanity; we are all connected. Whenever you think negatively of a fellow being, you hurt yourself.

This also implies to whenever you think positively. Your positive thoughts will create good energy, and this energy will manifest itself in a physical outer form. It will become real.

You create your life, your opportunities, and your actions from the very thoughts that you send out.

Evidently, you are more or less caught up in different

patterns of thought, patterns that place you exactly where you are now in your life.

This is where a great work begins, uncovering these patterns, so that they become recognizable to you, and you can change them in turn.

Recognize a pattern of thought that is harmful to you, and work with a conscious effort to change this.

You can say:

- I know now that this pattern of thought [specify which pattern you are thinking of] is harmful to me.
- I pray that it must be forgiven and absolved.
- I pray that I may think this instead: [specify new thought].

To clarify this method, we suggest that you call upon any deity or guardian that is especially helpful and benevolent to you. It could be God, Christ, the Holy Mother, Krishna, Allah, Buddha, the Great Spirit (or the Great Grandmother), the angels, or anyone who feels right for you when you are working with forgiveness. In this book, we have chosen God.

You then say, "God, I pray that you will forgive me this pattern [specify which pattern you are thinking of] and that you will neutralize and absolve its influence on my life and on me."

Here are some examples of patterns:

- God, I pray that you will forgive me of my pattern of comparing myself with other people.

- God, I pray that you will forgive me of my pattern of feeling nervous and afraid in relation to the coming time. I am asking for your help to feel stronger and rest more assuredly in the present.

To experience the full effect of conscious work with forgiveness, you must have an insight into the nature of how energy, emotions, and patterns of thinking create bonds between people and generations.

In order that the forgiveness can create release and purification, it is of the utmost importance that you understand who is sending you the emotion or thought in question, as seen in the understanding that all emotion and thought are circulation and stem from a certain place.

The people we grow up with influence us in a way that forms patterns of emotion, thought, and belief within us. As grownups, we must consciously work to separate this influence on an inner plane, in order to find our own nature in relation to the teaching that life has given us.

We cannot settle for asking forgiveness for ourselves, as full potential of forgiveness is only realized when we understand our lineage—our roots in our family—and that we ask forgiveness for the place in our family from where the negative emotion or thought arose.

The reason for this procedure is that you must fully realize that everything is circulating and that no specific person is to blame; everything is a common heritage, which, in turn, can be transformed into learning and wisdom.

When this understanding is in place, you will be able to free yourself from the patterns that hold you back and hamper the expression of who you are.

Example:

- God, I pray that you will forgive the pattern [specify which pattern], which I have from my mother, and redeem its influence. I pray forgiveness for whatever this pattern has created of emotions, judgments, or physical, psychic, and mental aspects in us both.

If a person knows that he or she has sent out negative emotions or thoughts, he or she can ask for forgiveness for what has been sent out and what it has created.

The mere understanding of from where things originate gives us redemption, but forgiveness is the final release.

In this, the circle of the pattern will be completed, and it will no longer affect your life and the choices you make.

This is a very direct and efficient way to recode your thought processes. Within a short time, you will experience a shift when you work with cleansing and forming yourself anew.

When the time is ripe, you will let go of the thought that has been tormenting you, and energy will be released for your next step in your development.

This is the way you have to work yourself through your body of thought.

It takes great patience because if you show impatience, your mind will cling to the old thoughts.

Patience toward yourself is of cardinal importance and is part of the love you must show toward yourself—the love and understanding you must constantly bestow upon yourself in this process.

> Forgive them, Father, for they know not what they do.
> —Luke 23:34

Working Sentences for "Thoughts"

- Thoughts create reality; thoughts are energy.
- Every negative or unkind thought you send out will come back and harm you. In this, you not only harm yourself but the combined karma of humankind.
- Uncover patterns of thought and change them.

Procedure

Example 1

- I know now that this pattern [specify which] is not productive for me.
- God, I ask that this must be forgiven and redeemed.
- God, I ask that, instead, I must think the following [specify new thought].

Example 2

- God, I ask of you to forgive me this pattern [specify which] and redeem and neutralize its influence on me and my life.

Concrete Examples

- "God, I ask you to forgive me this pattern of comparing myself with others."
- "God, I ask you to forgive me this pattern of feeling anxiety for the future. I ask for more confidence so that I may rest in the now."
- Work on understanding the pattern in itself and from where it originates, always realizing that all energy moves and comes from somewhere.
- Show that you respect your lineage and that the concept of guilt has no meaning.
- When you see a pattern arising from your parents, say, "God, I ask you to forgive the pattern [specify which] that I carry from my mom (or dad) and to redeem its effect on me. I ask for forgiveness for whatever emotions and judgments it may have caused in its physical, psychic, and mental aspects."
- In this way, you set yourself apart from others and find your own nature.

7

Your Ego

It is good for you to know that your mind—your ego—can get afraid when you start working on purifying and cleansing yourself.

In all reality and concreteness, your ego fears that you want to get rid of it. Your ego knows all your patterns in depth and is not fond of change.

In this, you must counsel with yourself—your ego. Soothe it and show that it is solely about evolving and that you now intend to use your contact to your higher self to a larger degree than before.

Sooner or later, your ego, your mind, will fall to rest and sense that nothing evil is afoot and that it only has to follow suit; that, in all actuality, it becomes an easier life for itself.

Your ego knows your fear and has controlled your life through this emotion until now, but it has to realize that life can be lived without fear in a higher dimension and that it is your choice to live in peace with yourself and the world around you.

But fear is strong, so this fear will be known to all, and it might control your life.

It will not help for us to say, "Fear not."

You must make the experience for yourself—that you have nothing to fear—when you surrender yourself to the divine aspect in you; when you recognize the value of your own spirit, your higher self.

Your higher self is connected with the spiritual and divine world, and when you allow the light and love from this world to stream down upon you on this earth, then fear will let you go, realizing that it has lost its battle.

You must have confidence in your own wish to channel light in this earthly realm in letting light manifest itself through you as a unique being, as a carrier of the light for whom the world is waiting.

Trust in the truth of your inner longing for light and love on earth because in this longing, you will see and feel your true *you*, the you created by God—shining, pure, and radiant.

Working Sentences for "Your Ego"

- Your ego may react with fear when you start working consciously with forgiveness.
- You must show that you want to have a stronger relationship with your higher self, rather than letting your ego control the course of your life.
- Your ego, in time, will rest assured and acknowledge the value and strength of your spirit so that you may surrender yourself to God.

8

Attacks on You as a Human

———

When you are attacked by another human being, the spiritual and karmic law still applies—that at some point earlier, you sent out thoughts of attack, and they have now boomeranged.

This could very well be from a former reincarnation, but since all your incarnations and all your experiences within those are contained in you, they are also a part of you.

This does not imply that you should let yourself face a barrage of insults and unkindness.

No, you must pull away, set a distance, and rest assured that you are now harvesting the learning invested in the attack to which you were subjected.

You must seek this learning—the message behind the occurrence.

What emotion or violation lies behind the attack?

Ask forgiveness for whatever is sent to you of these emotions, and you will neutralize its effect, as long as you perceive that this was once sent out by you.

By taking a distance to the part attacking you, you are protecting yourself—an act of love toward your own self.

And this is the point—harvest your learning in the opposition you meet and then pull away.

Most attacks, great or small, are met with counterattacks, possibly the worst solution to a conflict.

This only fuels aggression and self-righteousness, so the only thing left is revenge or claiming one's right.

In this way, any conflict becomes endless, until one party realizes the mechanism and pulls away, without having been satisfied.

In this respect, it will be a great help for the remaining party if the one who pulls away from the conflict can master praying to God for compassion and love for the one who remains.

This act is intensely provoking and disarming and will deny the remaining part the opportunity of further expressing his or her anger or frustration.

The remaining party, quite evidently, will feel utterly spent and become even more desperate, until he or she opens up to spiritual guidance—unless the remaining party perishes, by the simple circumstance that bitterness and holding a grudge are the most devastating emotions.

When an attack is pointed against you, or you simply feel you are being treated unjustly, you should know that we are ready to help you.

You must ask for our help in handling the conflict, and then ask us to show you the truth in your mutual experience.

Rest assured that you have passed on this issue to the right authority and that we will make sure that the person involved will get the experience necessary for his or her development at exactly the right moment.

In this way, you must also realize the importance of asking forgiveness for what others are sending out to you, be it emotional or thought-based.

You must understand the influence other people have on you, until you are able to see this clearly and reject what is being laid on you by others.

When you realize that a certain person thinks or feels something about you, then ask of him or her from us: forgive whosoever sends anger, sorrow, or likely things your way.

If you know for certain who is sending you concrete thoughts or emotions, do not hesitate to use the name of that person so that we can work in a more direct way.

But always remember that even in this, you are working on cleansing yourself and all of humanity in love.

In relation to attacks upon you as a person, sometimes you will need something more physical to reject an unjust provocation.

There are circumstances when people neglect or directly debase the spirit of a fellow human being that is the higher self of that person.

In this case, you must react, and things must be gainsaid. A very handsome way to do this is to write a letter to the person in question.

Tell him or her, in a written and correct manner, that your boundaries have been crossed and that you decline to be associated with the emotional or intellectual content of the attack.

Avoid expressions of anger or reaction; state your own worth as a human being and the fact that no human being can judge the value of another.

Thereby, you are delivering a spiritual lesson to the person implied, and it is up to that person to make use of it.

The difference between reacting with anger or responding with firmness is that the latter is much more constructive.

You are aligned with us when you are not personally telling someone off but living in correlation with the ethical rule, given to you by the spiritual realm; namely, that all human beings are equally important and have their own worth.

In a conflict, you must seek wisdom and knowledge in your own heart—the right action to take and which form this action implies.

It is important that you realize that the person attacking your values—your spirit, that is—does not respect his or her own values, neither spiritually nor as a human being.

You are showing this to the person in question, thereby helping a fellow human being to realize the connection between seeing oneself as a beautiful, living being, radiant in the light of the Creator, and knowing one's own worth.

Working Sentences for "Attacks on You as a Human"

- The law of karma applies: what you send out, you will receive, which implies that whatever you receive, you have, at one point, manifested.

- Seek for the deeper meaning and the message behind it.
- Receive your teaching and avoid the conflict.
- You may ask God to send light and love to the person with whom you disagree.
- Ask that we, from the divine hold, will show you the spiritual truth in your common experience.
- Understand that the thoughts and emotions that others carry for you have a deep impact on you.

Ask forgiveness:
"God, I ask you to forgive whoever may send feelings of anger, sadness, or other things to me."

- Remember that you are working for the love of the whole of humankind.
- If you experience anyone demeaning the spirit of another human being, it may give rise to you making a written statement, disclaiming the content of the attack.
- Make a distance and show your stance.
- By conflict: seek your wisdom in your inner world and realize that a person who demeans your spirit is not capable of acknowledging his or her own worth.

9

The Spiritual Search
of Human Beings

As mentioned earlier, everyone must seek the innermost core of their own souls in order to know themselves.

The core of the soul harbors the connection to the divine truth and the consciousness of being a divine being, which, in itself, indicates a higher truth than the one that human beings are pursuing in their lives at present.

The time has come when many people feel lonely and empty inside.

They feel a lack of connection or belonging, and they have realized that a relationship with others cannot fulfill these needs.

What is it that you are seeking?

Through many incarnations, you have lived solely through your interdependent relationships, but now, the time has come for you to realize that you need more than this to satisfy your needs—to feel that you belong and are connected to this life-world.

There is a great unrest among human beings, as you are not able to give to one another what you are seeking: your own relationship with the divine.

By focusing on letting other human beings fulfill your needs, you, at one time, will run dry and feel the emptiness.

There is a vacant space inside you that never has been filled, and many people know and dread this emptiness.

This is a cardinal point where many people surrender to the divine truth and ask for help.

You only have to pray for our help, and we will provide it.

This does not mean that we will intervene and remove every feeling of pain or unbalance, but we will help you live and learn through these experiences.

No one, not even us, can break the law of karma and therefore, you will experience that your human sufferings will continue, even though you have surrendered yourself to your inner truth, your divine relation.

The difference will be that you will have the ability to raise yourself above human suffering and see the broader view, and you will be able to work much more constructively with the assignments you have.

You will be given insight in the plan for your life, your destiny, and in time, you will harvest the understanding of why things occur and how they provide you with the experience you need.

Many would be greatly relieved if they could only see their lives as a task they themselves have set out to do.

You will be given assignments; you will experience, recognize, and widen your consciousness, which is needed to proceed in this life but also to accomplish your soul's journey through these human incarnations in this life-world.

When the light of understanding and recognition appears in your mind, you will attain the ability to affect your karma in a positive way. In any case, you will be able to avoid producing more darkness—bad karmic vibration that eventually will catch up to you.

Working Sentences for "The Spiritual Search of Human Beings"

- Many people feel they lack something and that mere human relations do not satisfy this need.
- This creates an empty space within that you can ask to have filled up.
- When you surrender to the divine truth, your suffering will not go away, but you will receive the help you need to go through karma and life.
- Karma cannot be lifted in an untimely fashion, but you will receive the ability to *life yourself above* suffering and torment and to see the broader view.
- This will provide an understanding of why things happen, and pain will ease with this insight.
- You will be able to see the plan of your life, learning to affect karma in a positive way by understanding and accepting what happens.

10

Suffering

Suffering is a man-made concept, in that every experience—every karmic incident—is a task that is placed on the way of the individual human being.

We know life is sometimes hurtful—that you feel pain, sorrow, and impotence; that life seems to go against you—but the greatest sorrow in your life comes from your belief that you have lost your connection to God.

It is paramount that you realize our willingness to help and that we are always eager to support the individual work of each and every one.

When you feel yourself ready to accept this invitation—when you feel it is time for your heart to open—then rest assured that every incident is a part of the divine plan for your life and that there is a deeper meaning behind everything.

Your task is to search for this meaning, to understand the reason why you were given these experiences and to extract the essence of every trial.

Accepting this will lead to human beings in growth, and this is the innermost wish of each and every individual.

11

Listen to Your Inner Voice

As you are now seeking and reading the message of this book, the divine truth will be laid open to you, layer by layer.

When you seek wisdom and truth around you, you will come to the realization that the specific truth and intimate relationship with the divine is to be found in the innermost heart of each and every person.

Then, you will experience that you must seek within yourself to establish the connection with God, which can fill your own inner emptiness.

The best teacher is to be found within yourself, for there, you have direct access to the higher truth, the divine truth.

You therefore must silence yourself, give yourself time, create peace, and avoid too many distractions in your attempt to contact your inner voice.

Your inner voice has been talking to you all your life, but you have not been able to hear it.

Now that you are consciously working on cleansing yourself, you will experience that you actually can hear this voice—the voice that fully knows you and always knows what is best and most right for you in any given situation.

Listen, listen, listen.

Be honest and serious, and write down what you are told. Write about your emotions, your thoughts, and your dreams.

Perhaps the meaning seems to be unclear at the moment, but when you look through your writing after a time, you will be able to see the thread leading through the maze, a plan of the events in your life, and you will regain confidence in your own inner world—your own inner voice.

The inner voice in each human being is directed and guided from the spiritual realm and, thus, is part of the divine truth.

You lost the trust in this fact long ago, but by working steadily, you will be able to regain this trust relatively fast, and it will be crucial for your development.

To see the search for individual development as egotistical is a great misunderstanding and a distortion of reality.

People often see only their own end, but the moment you seek spiritual development and are humble of heart, the urge to develop is for the good of all humankind.

Most people seek inner development from a deep urge to become free—free from human constraint and distortion—and everybody who sincerely embark on this journey toward a better life and a meaningful life not only help themselves but the whole humankind.

It is important to stress that everyone who purports

otherwise speaks from a place where the fear of losing control holds sway, as well as the fear of giving up power and the fear of the great unknown.

It will be the task of these people to realize that all true and loving humanitarian work departs from a pure heart, and a pure heart includes purification; to understand that helping others is only pure and honest when this help comes from an unselfish and loving heart, a heart that knows and understands human suffering; that by knowing and experiencing human suffering, each human being has experienced the spiritual laws of life; and by knowing them, they are capable of true compassion and love of others.

True help is given without any judgment or need to feel like a good person.

True help is given because the giver knows that it is the truth of God that human beings help one another to become conscious and ascend to a truer and clearer level of existence.

Only when each individual being has been fully cleansed will its attempts to help others become fruitful. The foundation of this is imperative: to give your inner-life attention and to give love and patience to yourself.

Only if you learn to give yourself these emotions will you be able to provide for others. If not, any attempt to help or heal others will eventually become mixed up with your own needs. You must take this seriously: give these important emotions to yourself before you give them to others.

If you do not start providing for yourself, sooner or later, your body or mind will remind you to do so by not functioning as you wish—and this will continue until you understand what it takes.

It takes love and respect for yourself.

When a you contact your inner voice, this voice will strengthen and develop you and the choices you make.

Again, you will be put to the test in this; you must learn to stand your ground, yet act lovingly in relation to people who do not understand.

The only thing to do is to pull away and elevate yourself above your feelings of not being understood or seen.

When first you have the connection to God, the acceptance and understanding of other people regarding your choices will matter little. It is vital that you do not succumb to letting the desires of other people control you or run your life.

This may feel lonely, but share with us, and you will experience that many people, all over the world, are faced with the same choice—heeding the apparent needs of others or heeding the needs of their own inner lives.

You are afraid to hurt others, but in your attempt to please, you only hurt yourself, and you stop your own spiritual development.

Acting according to your inner truth is never an unloving act. *Unloving* is dishonesty toward yourself and falsehood toward others.

It is a difficult test. Regardless of how others react, you must stand fast and hold your ground, resting assured that your inner voice knows the truth of what is best for you in any given situation.

Do not confuse this certainty with egotism. No, on the contrary, it is an act of love to all human beings—an important reminder to all human beings to be themselves too, taking full responsibility for their lives and actions.

Working Sentences for "Listen to Your Inner Voice"

- The truth is found in the heart of every human being.
- The best teacher is your own inner voice.
- Give yourself time and listen.
- Appreciate yourself by writing down your emotions, thoughts, experiences, and dreams.
- Regain confidence in your inner voice.
- Development is borne of the desire to be free.
- Your spiritual search is a help to all humankind.
- The best way to help others is to give with a pure and unselfish heart, which has been purified and thereby enabled to pass on divine love in an ethically sound way.
- Human suffering helps you to understand the spiritual laws of life.
- Love and patience are life-sustaining emotions that you must learn to give to yourself.
- When you rest in yourself, through having fulfilled your inner needs, you will be able to help others in an unselfish way.

- A person in spiritual training may change, and his or her surroundings may have a hard time keeping up with this change.
- Hold your ground, while showing love to others.
- Your loneliness as a seeking person can be amplified but only to direct your attention to the spiritual realm, from which you can ask for cohesion and support.
- It is never unloving to act from your inner truth.

12

Emotions

The decision to commence the task of uncovering your emotional life will forever change your life.

From this decision, you will realize that the responsibility for all your inner emotions rests within yourself, and you will not grasp for an outside cause or explanation any longer.

It is a big decision that has many consequences.

You will have to learn how to feel your emotions and how to give them the space and the time they need.

First and foremost, you must be willing to look at yourself and all the emotional conflicts you have, and then put these emotions in order.

For each emotion, you must understand its cause and what effect this cause has on you.

This will bring the foundation of your life in focus, as you are more or less living your life after the rule of your emotions.

This implies that if you have many supressed or negative emotions, the energy of these will stand in the way of your life.

You will experience yourself as blocked, as if there is a blockage in the system, and it is this blockage that you will need to soften up or dissolve.

When you react in a new way in a certain situation, this will show you that old emotional patterns are moving and call for attention.

You must note that such openings may seem a little hard the first time, until you get used to using your emotions in a new way.

Most people have suppressed feelings, and when you suppress a feeling, you turn it inward, instead of showing the world how you are feeling.

You might excel at this—until you hit the wall, where you cannot hold any more suppressed emotions within you.

There will be different reactions—you might become physically or mentally ill; you might become bitter and disillusioned; or you actually might meet your end this way.

At the same time, your supressed emotions are directed unconsciously to others, as they create energy that needs to be surcharged, in a way.

You actually damage the person you address in this way.

Sooner or later, you will have to claim the responsibility you have in this to the people around you.

Some people learn this by destroying themselves, by becoming naked and vulnerable.

This may be necessary before the seriousness of an unconscious emotional life becomes clear to you.

This is what is referred to as a nervous breakdown.

When your defense mechanisms fall, emotions surge upward from where they have been stowed away. Letting them into light may seem somewhat explosive.

It is important now that you decide to try to understand yourself and navigate in this ocean of emotions that suddenly appears before you.

It is like this: if an emotion appears, it is ready to be salvaged.

Treat it kindly and pray that you might work with this emotion in order to give you the experience that it set out to give.

As with patterns of thought, *forgiveness* is the key to closure in emotional questions.

When you sense that an emotion is holding you back, ask to have it forgiven:

"God, I am asking you to forgive me the emotion [describe or name it]. I ask you to forgive whatever this emotion may have caused."

Basically, this is enough.

Likewise, you may ask forgiveness for the pattern of anxiety you have—from your mother or father, for instance. Remember to ask forgiveness for whatever this might have caused you.

You can always ask for help and strength to replace these patterns with something better. We will never let you down.

Concerning suppressed emotions, it is also important to ask forgiveness in order to have their impact neutralized and abolished.

When you detect a suppressed emotion, which your inner journey of self-discovery will allow, then ask to have that emotion forgiven.

You can say:

"God, I ask you to forgive whatever suppressed emotions I may have: anger, frustration, or anxiety [here, you specify which]. I ask you to forgive what they may have created."

You have taken a major step when you dare to look at all the emotions without fear of being condemned or rejected for feeling something that is not allowed.

It is simply like this: emotions can never be illegal or wrong. All our emotions are there to teach us something about ourselves.

If you are afraid of the rejection of God, rest assured that God never condemns anyone who feels alone. God wants you to listen to and live by your inner wisdom.

The expression "being the master of your own house" expresses this truth—individuals take the full responsibility for their inner and outer lives and, in this way, take control of their own lives.

If all your suppressed emotions take control, then fear and anxiety get hold of you, and you lose your grip on your life.

Therefore, you must take this into your heart:

- Only by thoroughly working through your emotional life will you have the sufficient overview and surplus in your life so that you can work for God.

You are bound to learn to use your spirit and your wisdom in order to:

•   Raise yourself above these emotions.

Truly take control of your life, no longer letting emotions control you and the unfolding of your life.

Know that the work you are doing with forgiveness is the work of the spirit. You are hereby creating a possibility for your spirit to gain the upper hand and thereby gain the access to God's truth and wisdom as an active part of your own life.

In psychological terms, *projection* is the mechanism by which you recognize in others the emotions that you yourself have suppressed, thereby refusing to take responsibility for the emotions yourself.

To a certain degree, you will always feel more comfortable with seeing your own faults in others, but the moment you accept spiritual development, you will be stopped in your hunt for the faults of others, as things will turn on you and force you to focus on your own emotional life.

You should only applaud this because it will help you on your way.

Show us that you understand this by

•   no longer partaking in talking behind the backs of others, or
•   occupying yourself with the supposed problems or faults of others.

Try, instead, to direct conversation discreetly away from discussing and criticizing others—also in conversing with other people.

Perhaps you can search for the reason why this or that person is brought up in conversation, and then show that you understand why that person reacts as he or she does.

Remember that whenever you focus on the faults of others, there is an imbalance in yourself. This, however, never gives you the right to criticize others, unless the person has asked for your opinion; in that case, always be constructive and positive in your critique.

Otherwise, both parties are best served with silence.

Always seek the inner reason why a certain person or action irritates you and brings you out of balance.

Working Sentences for "Feelings"

- Uncovering your emotional life is a huge task.
- You must observe yourself, look inward, feel your emotions, and learn to understand them.
- Suppressed emotions block the unfolding of your life.
- New patterns of reaction show you that old emotions are moving and ready for closure.
- Suppressed emotions create energy that is unconsciously sent to others.
- Take responsibility for your emotions.
- Take a loving stance toward your emotions, and harvest the experience they carry for you.

- When you sense a feeling blocking you, ask to have it forgiven. Say, "God, I am asking you to forgive the emotion of _____ [specify the emotion in question]."
- When you become conscious of a suppressed emotion, ask forgiveness to have it neutralized and abolished. Say, "God, I am asking you for forgiveness for whatever emotions I may have suppressed—anger, frustration, anxiety [name the feelings that you are in contact with]."
- Feel free to describe the origin of the emotion, if you perceive it. For instance, you can ask forgiveness for the pattern you have of economic concern that you inherited from your mother. Ask forgiveness for whatever this concern may have created.
- Every emotion within you is there to help you to learn.
- Your emotions show you how you can learn to listen and live by your inner voice.
- Only by working through your body of emotions will you gain surplus in your life.
- You need your spirit in order to *raise yourself above these emotions* and see life from a new perspective. Then, you will take command of your life.
- Working with forgiveness is the work of the spirit.
- Projections and rejection of responsibility will stop when you confront your emotional life.
- See not the fault in others, but look into the cause for your irritation, and understand others from this point.
- When you see only the shortcomings of others, you are unbalanced yourself.

13

Family

Through your interpersonal relationships, you often are entangled in a way that can take years to disentangle.

It is a vast task that asks you to be just like you are, especially with the ones closest to you. The reason is that you have bound each other up in family ties and yearly traditions of how it is supposed to be and who is supposed to do what. You have roles to play that are undefined, and you play along as long as best you can.

You will harm yourself before you break the unspoken rules and the expectations of how you perform as a real member of your family.

The bottom line is that there is no right or wrong with regard to how a family is supposed to look or how the members perform their roles.

When a person decides to break these rules or simply to do things in another way than the rest—say, by doing something unexpected—the reaction can be fear and discomfort—fear of novelty, fear of change, fear of its consequences.

A lot of people try to conform to a family pattern created long ago through different generations and that governs the life of family members—a pattern created by fellow humans, not by God.

It was never God's intention that you should control and manipulate each other to the extent of what is happening. Through the message of this book, please set each other free.

To reach this end, you will have to work outside your comfort zone because this is where you will be challenged when you consciously determine to set each other free.

This does not mean that you cannot have intimate relations; on the contrary, when you face your fear of losing, you will engage in more direct and closer relationships.

Your family is only on loan, so to speak; it is the framework you need in order to get born.

A mother and a father come together in order for you to have a point of departure.

When the norms and values of your earthly parents create a web, and you get caught up with human emotions and the fear of losing, what fails you is the ability to stand your ground.

Leaving home and the expectations of your mother and father can be a burden on your shoulders. Actually, you ought to fly like a bird from the nest, but far too often, your wings have been broken, and you lack the courage.

Many grown-ups take the need and opinion of others into account, while trying to lead their lives and trying not to hurt the feelings of those closest to them.

But the one closest to you is God, and the only one you can hurt—by not following the road appointed to you by God—is you.

It is a common misunderstanding that taking care of yourself leads to the neglect of others. If this happens, it is because the party involved had something to learn and ought to be grateful for the teaching.

In other words, what might look like an unloving act may turn out to be the greatest gift of love, just because the giver has realized that every single human being must claim responsibility for his or her own life—and only for this.

Through their actions, this is made manifest to the ones closest to the person changing.

This is not to be confused with the responsibility for the children of whom we have been given the care.

Our children walk in our footsteps, and our responsibility is to show them acceptance and freedom to be their own true selves.

We can never ask anything in return for the work of bringing up children, as this is a special privilege given to us by God. The greatest honor and the greatest gift are to give birth and then to raise the children.

With this said, it is important that you realize, deep in your heart, that your own parents were chosen for exactly the qualities they have, in order for you to evolve as a soul. In this, you must respect your lineage, whatever its cause.

Understand this: if you judge and disrespect your parents, you judge and disrespect yourself. You must always see your parents as a source of revelation to your own nature so that you can get to know yourself by understanding your parents and your family in this life.

Your earthly family is only borrowed for the time being. Your true family is your spiritual family, where everyone is united in God and ordered into families, connected by spiritual relationships, creating support and strength between souls.

Listen to this divine truth: all are equal, and no one can expect anything from another, and no one has to answer to anyone, except to God.

Working Sentences for "Family"

- The family is the place of many expectations and yearly traditions; the individual members try to conform to these.
- The will of God is that you will let each other develop, side by side; this may cause anxiety.
- Close relationships become more authentic if each party takes responsibility for himself or herself and avoids manipulating others.
- Many people struggle to serve the needs of others and themselves.
- Serving your own needs does not hurt others.
- By living and acting from your own inner space, you show the ones closest to you how each individual must take responsibility for himself or herself.

- Responsibility for your children is something else; accept them and give them the freedom to be themselves.
- It is a gift and an honor to raise children.
- Parents are chosen for the quality that the soul needs in order to develop.
- You must always respect your ancestors.
- If you pass judgment on your parents, you judge yourself. Your parents are a source of understanding and knowledge about you.
- Everyone is equal; no one can expect anything from others; no one is responsible or has to answer to anyone but God.

14

Fear of Losing

Your fear of losing manifests itself in all aspects of your life—in your human relations and certainly also in your relationship with material goods.

Know this truth in your heart: all fear of losing comes from the experience of losing contact with the divine and sensing that your connection to God is lost; that is, thinking that you lost contact with God.

This pain is reflected every time you lose something you care for, and in this way, you are kept in a game of dependency.

This is a game known to you through many reincarnations, and you are so immersed in it that you cannot picture yourself happy and complete without the usual people and things around you.

Every human being is, to a certain degree, dependant on his or her surroundings, if the inner dialogue is missing and does not produce inner confidence. You seek confidence in the outer world through other people and material goods.

In this, you have generated a pattern of mass

consumption on earth that is causing instability and unrest in the ecosphere, as well among human beings on earth.

The confidence and comfort you seek among other human beings and through material goods will never match the one you really need—the confidence of knowing that God loves you and gives you unconditional love.

The pain of being cut off from this inner dialogue with God is so great that you had to turn away from the truth— that you yourself turned your back to God in your power-driven and self-righteous attitude and that you are now afraid to look God in the eyes.

Understand that God's only wish is for you to turn to God and to receive the healing, light, and love that God is offering you.

God forgives you, but the real question is, can you forgive yourself? This is the only boundary between God and you.

You must learn, once again, to feel worthy of God, and you can only do this by cleansing yourself and your doings on earth.

God never left you; you turned your back on God and the divine rules, but God was there all the time, in all times, following you carefully. God is always ready to open up the inner connection to you, the inner dialogue.

God never gave up and never will give up on you.

God's aim is to make you open your heart and rediscover the divine path inside.

God's work is to lead you unto truth and to the wisdom needed for you to be a worthy bearer of divine light on earth.

As it is, many souls on earth, at this very time, open up

their hearts to receive a seed for a new life, with a spiritual dimension as yet unknown to you.

You are reaching out for God's light, and this provides God with possibilities in his ways of shedding light on earth and, thus, healing the wounds of darkness and destruction.

This little seed of hope and the opening of your hearts is the prerequisite for you to obtain wisdom and rediscover the ethics of divine rule and strain to live by it.

Working Sentences for "Fear of Losing"

- All fear of losing is merely a recollection of losing your divine connection.
- Fear of losing creates dependency.
- Dependency is outer comfort in place of inner peace and confidence.
- Comfort and confidence in relation to others can never replace the confidence of knowing that God loves you.
- God forgives you, but can you do the same? Can you forgive yourself?
- After cleansing yourself, you can feel worthy of God.
- God never left you. You turned your back on God and the divine rule.
- God works for you to open your heart.
- Many souls, in this day and age, open up their hearts.
- This opening is the basis for wisdom and of living according to the divine rule.

15

Time for Inner Life

———————

Along with your inner soul-searching, it is important that you make time for yourself.

Human beings have forgotten the meaning of looking inward and seeking the tranquility and wisdom of an inner life.

In order to rediscover your inner life, you must create vacant periods of time in your life, where no one or nothing can make demands on you.

It does not have to be hours, as long as you give your inner self your full attention.

This may prove difficult to you, as you have created a hectic everyday life, where everything is entangled, with no natural time for inner contemplation.

This proves itself through the fact that many people have a hard time concentrating and being grounded, sometimes feeling uprooted and meaningless as they endeavour to lead the good life.

It is of utmost importance that you take time to find peace and quiet to go into silence. Without it, your spiritual and human development will seem just as uprooted and vain as your actions to secure material gain.

Realize that it is much nicer for you to be in close contact with your inner life, to have your finger on the pulse, so to speak, so that you are not overrun when your emotions suddenly force you to recognize what is going on inside you.

Sometimes this wake-up call comes in a sudden way, but it can be necessary in order for you to awake.

This will happen sooner or later, as you will not be able to supress your emotions throughout your entire life.

If you choose this solution, know that you are degrading yourself, and this was never God's wish for you and your unique life on earth.

Starting out, peace can be hard to find, especially because you think it takes a certain demand. You will have to learn to let go of control and relax.

Many people feel the noise of their surroundings, and it can be hard to tolerate these noises.

This confrontation with your busy life shows you how scary the silence can be.

Letting your thoughts and emotions flow freely and giving your mind a space for quiet can be a major task for you. But if you are serious about cleansing yourself, you must accept this truth: that without inner stillness, you won't find your way to God, and all your endeavours to find the path will be in vain.

Remember, above all, to treat yourself with respect, patience, and love because this is the key to your happiness.

Understand that the reason why more and more people

live their lives with quiet time in their daily routines is that this is the way to their core, to the place where they belong, and from where everything else takes its departure.

Do not hesitate; start showing God—and yourself—that you are ready to bring yourself into greater balance by using the tools you have been given.

Working Sentences for "Time for Inner Life"

- Find time for inner contemplation—each day, if possible.
- Take time without demands or expectations, just silence; fifteen minutes will do.
- Sit down; feel your inner world.
- Sense how you are feeling.
- Without stillness, you cannot find the path to God, and all your efforts will be in vain.
- Through this time, you will find your inner core.

16

The Word of God

From ancient times, many misunderstandings and misinterpretations of God's Word have occurred.

Human beings laid out the truth and wisdom of God in their own words, and the more times things were told, the more rewriting of the truth occurred.

Some human beings, thinking that they were delivering the gospel, unconsciously got their own egos mixed up with the words of wisdom, and other human beings were misled.

In later days, the written word gained in importance, and people forgot *to go into themselves and consult their inner truth* and knowledge of God.

As it is stated, the Word of God is the law, but do not assume that old texts, delivered over and over by human beings, always correspond to the truth of God.

What humanity is lacking is seeking its own connection to God, rather than solely leaning on a preacher or written source, who might partake in the truth but which is, nevertheless, rounded by human influence and error.

Certain aspects of divine truth have been deprived of

humanity in your obsession with the written word. You have taken words literally, instead of trusting your own inner voice and developing your own tools of understanding in each case.

What is lacking is the deep recognition that every human is unique, that each has his or her own inner truth and connection to the divine, and this means that you cannot generalize as you have done.

You underestimate yourself when you see yourself as one gross population, following the same line of so-called progress, without regard to karma and the individual plan for each human being that was laid down by God and that very human being.

Of course, you share the same experience and life-world, but the tempo and succession in your development is only for God's perspective and judgment to see if it is aligned with the truth.

Some people obediently follow one or another interpretation of God's wisdom, thereby forgetting their own part in the puzzle, their own truthful connection with God.

Powerful and intense souls might run you over in instructing you how to believe.

In this way, you hand over your own initiative, your discrimination, to others, and you forget to feel the truth deep within yourself.

These words are a loving reproof to all to take responsibility for finding the truth and not only to listen to the words of how others have found it.

Of course, you can accept and receive guidance and teaching from others but hold on to the one truth that your own heart will tell you—the true valour of what is being presented to you.

Human beings will always seek and be in need of knowing the truth; in this, you have a deep and primordial knowledge, which is the source of everything, and all causes-and-effects depend upon this truth being fulfilled.

This realization might not be conscious to you, but in this very time, there is great turmoil around this aspect of life, and we find it is time for you to receive further knowledge and information as to your path as humanity.

Rest assured that you will be shown the way, and by receiving this knowledge, your heart already has accepted the development you seek; namely, to be more conscious of your spiritual dimension, as a human being on your soul's journey, as well as in your daily life.

Working Sentences for "The Word of God"

- The Word of God has often been misinterpreted or mixed with the ego or power greed of human beings.
- You have forgotten to seek your inner truth.
- You are missing the realization that each person holds his or her own truth and is governed by the law of karma.
- Maintain your own sense of judgment and the responsibility for your own truth, which is part of the divine truth.

- *Seek in your own heart*, and receive guidance and teaching from there.
- Humanity is ready to receive more information on the tasks you face.

17

Faith and Trust

———

Dear brothers and sisters:

You who choose to walk the path of light will be tested on your faith, trust, and humbleness.

Do not fear these challenges, as they have been measured out to you and your development, showing new ways and new sides of your countless resources and potential.

You will never face a challenge for which you do not hold the resources or tools to manage, if only you listen and act according to your spirit and its knowledge of truth and wisdom.

Approach life without fear, always praying to God, the heavenly entity, to hold you—not that you are turning down responsibility for your own life but rather that you are asking for support from God.

The highest confirmation of faith is when you know, deep inside, that you are doing your best to fulfill this work as it was meant to be, letting it be up to God that this will come true.

In this manner, put your fears aside, saying, "I am ready

for this challenge, and I am praying for you to make the right happen."

In this manner, lay down your desire to control things or to always to plan the next step. Accept that only God holds the key to future events and the knowledge of what serves everybody in the best of way, in this specific case.

You must never forget that behind each happening rests a truth and a meaning that is deeply connected to that point in time—a causality of the heart, open to anyone who dares to see.

Remember that any so-called problems or obstacles you meet on your way are only assignments, given to you in order to strengthen and purify you, in order to grow into the bearers of light who will be needed in relation to the big work of cleansing that lies before all.

Working Sentences for "Faith and Trust"

- Those who choose the path of light will be tested on their faith, trust, and humbleness.
- These challenges will always match your level of development, and you will not be faced with something you cannot handle.
- The biggest confirmation of faith is when you let the will of God rule.
- In this, you let go of control and let trust grow.

18

Consciousness

The main theme of this book is purification and cleansing.

The cleansing of the individual human being is the prerequisite for spiritual growth. The growing self-awareness of the spirit will only come through as a clear channel, when introspection and individual soul-searching has occurred.

Being made conscious of your spirit will not make everything smooth and painless, but you will be able to recognize how the ethical laws work and the great extent to which the spiritual realm is connected with earth and humanity.

As you progress with your cleansing and inner purification, you will chance to meet great challenges, in relation to others, in an array of circumstances.

You will have to learn to be led, rather than taking the lead, almost as if you were watching your life from the outside.

This will be possible because you will see the connections of your life—how it is formed by cause-and-effect.

This does not imply letting go of responsibility for what

happens; rather, it's the opposite. Know that everything that happens in your life stems from you and that you are experiencing exactly this because you are ready to face the message it carries for you and the overall plan for your life.

Know that nothing in this world is by chance.

Everything absolutely has a purpose and a given meaning.

This means that you can go into any occurrence or relationship and analyze wherein lies the teaching for you at any given moment. You will experience the satisfaction and comfort of understanding the connection and causality of your life and thereby be able to carry even the burden of painful experience.

Nothing in your life happens by chance, even though it often looks like that.

Understand that behind everything lies a truth from God, and nothing is meaningless, pointless, or futile.

Futility and meaninglessness are man-made concepts to cover up the naked truth of cause-and-effect, showing human beings where they have given away their responsibility.

Also, claim this responsibility and become a free spirit, as a whole human being, recognizing that all comes from God in truthful correlation with his plan.

Some people always make designs for their lives, planning each event and detail. They consider every eventuality, turning every possibility in their minds, always trying to avoid the unforeseen.

The complex relationship of karma laws, however, will often throw aside your designs, making your life seem unpredictable. Your existence is traversed by energies that need accounting for, maybe stemming from previous lives. You cannot overlook or control these forces that seek equilibrium, as it is not yours to control.

You can control, however, the karmic account of the future by cleansing yourself and acting from a compassionate heart, but you will never be able to control karma and the destination of your life journey.

You are deluding yourself with thought patterns of anxiety and your desire to control events that are out of your hands, to a degree, where you become unnatural and deranged in your attempt to halt karma and predetermine events.

You lose the ability to live in the present and fully enjoy it as it is.

You forget to suck in the intense feeling of happiness of each passing moment when you constantly project yourself into your concern about the future.

This simply does not support any meaningful goal.

Instead, you will become strung out and bogged down because you lose your spontaneous joy of life by being occupied with what will happen tomorrow or in ten minutes.

You carry an unconscious anxiety for the unknown, and you would like to prepare yourself for all eventualities because you have lost faith in the fact that God lets everything happen and works in his own ways.

You forget how to float along and see the plan for your life unfold in the most beautiful way.

It does *not* mean that you are only along for the ride and that God will steer the car for you. No, you must pay attention, stay focused, and act when necessary or when you are called.

You must be active in your life. Remember that you carry the responsibility to lead your life and live your life. God cannot do that for you.

In order to feel the rhythm of life, which has been given to you by the spiritual world, it is important that you can listen to your own inner voice.

It is from this source that you will receive answers, impulses, and inspiration to act and work in communion with your nature. This is the higher purpose with your life here on earth: to stay in alignment with your higher self.

To enable these impulses and messages to act and work through the different layers of your physical body, your psychic body, and your energy body, you must again realize the importance of cleansing yourself.

You must make up your mind as to where your intensity will be most focused—in the inner or the outer life—and then start working consciously on reflecting on your life and your actions.

By outer life, we mean everything that is oriented outside you.

The outer life is focused on physical matters—the body and its appearance. It is centered around activities like consumption and experiences of satisfaction of the fleeting moment, without time for inner reflection.

The outside life is not concerned with cause-and-effect, only with satisfaction and sensory fulfillment, which, in turn, produce a culture that is not only centered on enjoying the moment but on seeing all things as vehicles or objects of this enjoyment. People use each other, in the moment, as agents of pleasure, without establishing a real and deeper contact.

The outside life that stands alone, without inner reflection, seems to us like escapism.

Fleeing from the truth of life, fleeing from intimacy, fleeing from nearness, and—although this is what everyone seeks—fleeing from *love*.

At a point in time, this vacuum created by the outer pursuit will materialize for you as an utter emptiness and feeling of disgust with yourself.

What is lacking in your outward-orientated life is true intimacy and interest in what each unique human being brings. Without empathy and compassion, it is easy to get lost.

You must understand that this compassion is not only given by others; in its purest form, it comes from God, if you are willing to open up yourself.

God never judges, never excludes, and always is ready to accept you, regardless of the life you have lived and the actions you have performed.

The moment you turn yourself toward God, you will receive help and support. This will be given to you. In this, there is certainty.

Your greatest challenge in this is actually that you think yourself unworthy of God's interest and your grief that you have lost connection with the divine.

You must realize your mistake in this regard: You have

misinterpreted and lost confidence; you have turned away from God, not the other way around.

Therefore, God is sending helpers and carriers of light to earth to help us to cleanse and purify the earth, so that the danger of perishing and laying earth bare as a waste will cease, and God's plan for the salvation of earth will come true.

Have courage, friend. Open up to the messages that are coming to infuse you with hope and inspiration for the great work that we have commenced together.

Working Sentences for "Consciousness"

- Consciousness will not liberate you from pain, but it will let you see the ethical laws of human life on earth.
- You will know cause-and-effect.
- Everything that is happening to you has its source in your own self.
- Cause-and-effect will let you see the structure and meaning of your life, and you will be able to see the meaning of what is happening to you. This will ease your pain and suffering.
- Nothing is without meaning.
- With anxiety and control, you lose your ability to live in the present.
- You can never steer or control the cause of events through your fear of the unknown.

- Anxiety makes you suffer and lose your joy of life.
- The plan of God will unfold as soon as you let go of control and fear.
- Do not be passive but focused and ready to step into action.
- In order to be aligned with your life rhythm, you must be able to receive impulses and inspiration and feel in your heart what is of importance to you.
- Outer life is not about cause-and-effect.

Standing alone, outer life is a hollow shell, an escape from divine love of life.

- Compassion and interest from God are the most real things you can get.
- Humanity itself has turned away from God.
- Therefore, God has sent helpers and light-bearers to earth who are helping you cleanse the darkness and create balance on earth.

19

Self-Judgment

Oh, cherished reader, take this to the innermost chamber of your heart:

So much love and optimism are flowing to you from the spirit realm. You are worthy to receive this and to work on the divine plan of God, as long as you show your goodwill and capacity with a true face.

In this, it is of the utmost importance that you are willing to look at yourself in the big mirror, where nothing is hidden—the big mirror, where everything surfaces, to be released and come forth in a much clearer and beautiful shape.

Do not be afraid of yourself and your own depth because this is what makes you a unique creature, made from the love of God. Look upon yourself with mild and loving eyes because the only release is in this.

If you scrutinize yourself with critical eyes, you will not be able to see or greet others with love and tolerance. Even if you might think that you are doing so, this is only vanity.

As long as you criticize yourself, you will also criticize others in the same way—perhaps in a hidden and secret way, but when this comes to the fore, the shallowness of your tolerance toward others will be obvious. You will never be able to *see* others as long as you do not recognize yourself.

Remember our words at the beginning of this book: the first key to spiritual growth is to see yourself with loving and patient eyes, whatever challenges and life lessons you are facing. However impossible those challenges and lessons may appear, always remember to look upon yourself with love.

Show us that you are holding the high ground in regard to whatever result you are now harvesting from your own actions, as long as you remember that the will of God is unfolding and that God looks upon you with immense love and mildness, wherever you may have taken yourself. God knows the relationship between you and what you have experienced in life, and he will help you so that the truth of the divine plan can become clear to you.

Working Sentences for "Self-Judgment"

- Everyone is worthy of working for God.
- Show goodwill and passion, and look honestly upon yourself so that you can be salvaged and appear more beautiful and cleaner than before.
- *Look upon yourself with mildness and love.*
- Criticism toward yourself will taint your view of others.
- The key to spiritual development is to look upon yourself with loving eyes.

20

Fear

Fear is your worst enemy, if you allow the concept of enmity as fear created by you.

When humanity lost its trust in its own inner spiritual connection with God, and thereby let the control of its life slip from its fingers, fear developed as the strongest and most destructive emotion it knows.

Fear halts you in all development; fear can literally drive you mad.

If you let fear get hold of you, it will tear every single bit of sense and sensibility out of you. You will have surrendered to a destructive force in the service of the dark power, which has enslaved you throughout the centuries and kept you away from the light of divine truth.

You are challenged, faced with the task of confronting your fear. Hold up the mirror and show your fear that it is time to let you go, to let humanity go, so that all may reunite with their Creator, the Almighty, who shaped you in *her* own image, the image of love that we call God.

What might actually happen?

Lose your family?

Lose the ones closest to you?

Lose your friends?

Lose your job?

Lose material goods?

Lose your money?

The worst possibility of all must be to lose yourself, your connection with God, your existence and purpose in life in this world.

When human beings lose hope—their vital spark of life—occurrences of life and death seem unbearable and inhuman, and they blame God for being a vindictive and punishing God, all the while wondering how it is possible to carry on.

When you end up here, you have one of two choices:

- Reconnect with the divine through your inner voice.
- End your life and be utterly spent.

If the second option is your choice, your road will only be longer. God will make another attempt to come into your life, with new karmic assignments and challenges for you to step up in the next life.

So, beloved human being, hold your ground, whatever the challenge may be, and know that the one who created you has a purpose for you, whether it is known to you or not.

At any time, you may turn your face to the light and pray to the Lord to take your hand and guide you through your inner voice, showing you your own wisdom and ability to live in concordance with God and divine truth, which, in time, will be the truth spoken on all of earth.

Working Sentences for "Fear"

- Fear is a human construct.
- Fear is the most powerful destructive emotion we know.
- Fear will stop your development and hold enormous power over you.
- The worst possible thing to happen is when you lose your sense of purpose in life.
- When you lose hope, you lose your vitality, and everything turns dark.
- Then, you have only one of two choices: reconnect with God, or perish.

21

Rootedness

———

Dearly beloved human beings:

As the wind sweeps leaves off the trees in fall, you sometimes swirl around in this life-world, trying to grab hold of its mysteries and higher meaning.

You search hither and thither. You are thrown around by the forces of your karma, but it is the opposite that you are longing for—feeling that you hold your power, setting the course of your own life, and steering clear of confusion.

You are blown away by the occurrences of life, forgetting to feel the grass underneath your feet and the solid rock of Mother Earth, trying to fly high in the spiritual domain without having secured your foundation in your own grounding and your way of life.

Perhaps you gain some small insight or nugget of wisdom, or maybe you readily access the vibration of higher planes, but without grounding in your own life, to what use will you put this knowledge?

You will only end up longing for freedom and strength of spirit, and the experience you harvested will come to nothing.

Accept that you are here on earth, situated here and now, and that your grounding must be for real.

You hail from heaven and the creative power of God, but as long as you are here on earth, it is precisely the balance between heavenly wisdom and earthly grounding with which you must come to terms.

It is the greatest test for human beings—to accept earthliness, while at the same time opening up and living in clarity and consciousness, clarity of spirit, and the ability to bring the quality of the spiritual into earthly life.

This is where many hesitate. After many trials, you realize your situation and hand yourself over to God in the form of your higher self. It is a bit like a purgatory, as you will experience that your ego and higher self can spend a lot of energy discussing who will lead, but when the ego realizes that it can let go of fear and despair, it also will realize that the strong emotions that have filled it almost to the breaking point can be transformed into a higher form of energy; namely, spiritual power and strength.

Thereby, the ego will enjoy a much greater freedom, having left the big task of steering the course to the higher self; namely, to lead and guide you through the ordeals of life.

The ego holds your personal experience of life on earth through this life only, and thus, it has a limited outlook.

The higher self brings the total sum of experiences from all lives and holds the promise for each unique individual to develop, according to the plan of God.

Here are facts that are often overlooked:

- The ego is of paramount importance for you to be grounded on earth.
- Without the ego, you would be like a ship without ballast, without the ability to participate in life.

The higher self cannot live life on earth alone in the human vehicle. All parts are necessary, and it is the ego that provides substance for human existence.

Therefore, you must give respect and dignity to your ego and cooperate, rather than fight it, in the inner process of handing over leadership from the ego to the higher self and, thus, be aligned with the divine truth.

Use your inner light and your love to make your ego realize that you can and will set it free. Ask that it follow your directions, which will only benefit the whole of you and create harmony and balance.

Do not ever think that you can do without your ego because it is here that all your earthly and human experience from this present life is stored, and from here, you draw your knowledge and understanding of humanity at its present state of development.

Working Sentences for "Rootedness"

- By searching hither and thither, you are thrown off balance.

- You lose control in your desire to elevate yourself.
- You need grounding here on earth to balance the energies of heaven and earth.
- You must become conscious of the higher self, bringing the qualities of the spirit into earthly life.
- Purification gives you inner clarity and makes possible the grounding that is a prerequisite for balance.
- Both the ego and the higher self are important for balance in human life, since the ego contains personal experiences, and the higher self contains experiences of the soul.
- Between these—ego and higher self—heaven and earth meet in each single individual, and you must respect each one in order to find balance and harmony.

22

Seeking Goodness

———

In seeking to become a good person, you must understand the essence of this—the right meaning.

A good person lives in a clean heart, humble in front of God, always perceiving the divine and, hence, positive aspect—in all situations.

Nothing exists in which God is not present. God is in everything, even in what appears ugly and evil.

There is a meaning behind everything, and human beings must arrive at the understanding and acceptance that God is in all, present in all.

God has no form but will always be present in the shape of light—the light of divine love—and always, no matter how dark it seems, there will be a small flame or ember that you can breathe into life.

The light of God is present in all, and you will be able to bring this forward with the right understanding and treatment of a given situation or circumstance.

This means that you will have to look for goodness everywhere, be positive, and work to create peace and oneness between human beings and your surroundings.

Too many people dwell on separation because of fear and lack of knowledge.

The feeling of separation destroys the human feeling of oneness. You become each other's jailers, and you find it hard to wish for the good of all and everyone around you.

Seek in your heart, and know that in here lies the seed to create the goodness you were meant to manifest—the good that will be victorious; the will of God come true; human karma released and elevated to the divine truth that God has set out for you.

As you work to see goodness in everything, work to seek goodness as the first and most sacred in any thought, feeling, and action and in every word.

As you always seek to promote goodness, point to goodness, and in your inner work, be so advanced that you enable yourself to feel and think goodness.

Your inner work, again, is the cleansing that is the foundation of your way of living.

If you wish from a pure heart, then deliver yourself to God and to the divine plan—the ultimate good. Then purify yourself and raise yourself by the power of light, that you may benefit God and human beings alike.

Working Sentences for "Seeking Goodness"

- God is in everything and you must seek the good in everything.

- God is on Earth in the shape of light, the light of divine love.
- There is always a spark of light that you can blow into life
- Separation destroys your feeling of being one, and goodness becomes hard to find.
- Seek into your heart because here is the seed of love, of goodness.
- Goodness must be the primary in all thoughts, emotions, acts and words.
- Emphasize goodness, point to it.
- Purify yourself and lift yourself by the power of light.

23

The Opening

————

When a person seeking the truth opens his or her heart, it is very important to find the core of divine truth—that everyone is equal and that all serve God.

Serving God will become a conscious activity that every individual will seek. The end of this will be to serve others and, by serving others, to serve God. This will have no other end, no other goal.

Too many people work from the desire for material goods or selfish ends. It is important to realize the following in your heart:

- See God in everything.
- Know that by carrying out your work, with love of human beings and God alike, you are serving God, and the selfish aspect will disappear as you dedicate your work and the profit you harvest to God.
- Working for God will take obedience and humbleness, as God does not accept fake dedication.

From a clean heart, you must wish to see any occasion to give to others as a gift from God—as a possibility for you to serve and be near God.

The love of God will stream through you, and your work will reach a new level of accomplishment, that you are letting the light of God shine through everything you do.

It is important for everyone to realize that without God, they cannot accomplish much. God is in everything and is omnipresent.

God is present for everyone who earnestly and humbly asks for help to do the task at hand.

When you realize that love is important, in coming to terms with yourself and your work, then your heart will open up for this love. It will be possible for you to cherish any encounter with others and lay your love in these meetings.

Soon, you will realize that it is the love of God doing the work, and you will experience a far deeper satisfaction with your existence.

Every chore in life will overflow with divine love, and it will seem an honor to do this work.

Working Sentences to "The Opening"

- Opening up your heart will make you realize that everybody is equal and that all are servants of God.
- Serving God will become a conscious task.
- See God in everything.

- When you carry out your work with the love of God and respect for others, the selfish aspect will disappear.
- Without God, individuals can achieve nothing.
- Love is important for coming in unison with yourself and the tasks in your life.

24

Grounding

As you know, the *rootedness* that we have spoken about in relation to earth is also called *grounding*.

The importance of this grounding cannot be emphasized enough in relation to human development.

It is important to understand what *grounding* means in your life and how you obtain it.

Grounding means that you have both feet solidly planted on earth in your daily life and that you are not constantly floating around in thoughts without focus.

Too many people use too much of their time and energy in simply holding on to their balance in life and relating to the outer stress to which they expose themselves.

It means that a lot of useful energy is lost in the mere attempt of keeping up with your own life.

The challenge for human beings is that grounding comes from inner peace, as well as leading a peaceful and simple life.

Many people are extremely busy, but when asked about it, they really don't know why. Perhaps you do not know but are merely trying to cope and keep up, thereby forgetting the true values in life that were meant for you to cherish and heighten in gratefulness for living in the divine light, with the light of God in your heart.

Grounding, or rooting, is obtained by stopping for a moment, listening to the impulses of earth itself, working steadily to gain more balance and time, wondering, and investigating what your inner life contains.

All outdoor pursuits—in nature, in the garden, with the materials of nature—will be good for your grounding. You will find a simple and wonderful peace by acknowledging how much nature means to you and how important it is to live in unison with her and her energies.

Just to *be*—simply be in nature—and to rest your eyes on the wonders of nature; to really see leaves, beetles, moss, and water; to really listen to the birds and the grasshoppers is pure bliss for the soul and will always comfort you.

At the same time, your place in your working life will give you grounding.

It is important that you go to your daily chores with happiness and joy, not with disgust and fatigue, because your working life holds the greatest source for peace and balance in your life.

It is important that you carry out your work with happiness and joy, that you understand the value in doing exactly the work you are supposed to do, that you realize there is a higher purpose to all jobs and work situations, that they each, in turn, are meant to teach you something, and that there are no coincidences.

Of course, your time may be spent in a given place and situation. Then remember to let go of fear and material concerns, and orient yourself toward your next journey in life.

Please never forget that God is paving the way for you, supporting you. Especially if you open up yourself to listening to the divine voice through your higher self, you will feel the guiding force leading you on your way.

Rest assured that you are always at the right place in time and space, and if you feel it is time to move on, follow your impulse, and uphold your agreement with God to develop, according to the plan that has been laid out for you.

Working Sentences for "Grounding"

- It is imperative that you have both feet solidly grounded in daily life on earth.
- You are spending too much energy on keeping your balance, due to your busy life.
- Grounding comes from leading a simple life.
- Stop and listen to the impulses of Mother Earth.
- Spend time wondering and studying your inner life.
- Nature gives balance. Accepting your bond with nature gives grounding.
- Listen to nature—the wonderful details, the peace.
- Your working life grounds you on earth. It gives you stability.

- Go to your assignments with joy. It will bring peace to your life.
- If joy is lacking, you must find the cause, and change it.
- Remember that you are in the right place at the right time.

25

Feeling Lonely

So many people across the world know the feeling of loneliness—deeply rooted loneliness and isolation, a terrible feeling that maims you and makes you suffer.

Even if you are in a large group, this deep loneliness can take hold of you, and you ask yourself, "How can this be when there are so many other people around?"

The company of other people only means that you are not alone. Loneliness is something else and is deeply situated in each human being. There is only one way out—the road leading to God.

When we feel this loneliness and let it torment us, it is because we have reached a time when we recognize that we can no longer live to be something for someone or to live through the experience and feelings of another human being.

Something is lacking, something essential and vital—the life force itself.

This is the realization that God lives in every one of us and always is there if we call, in silence—call and wait.

In silence, God resides, and from silence, God receives your prayer.

Through your heart and through your higher self, you will establish a connection to the divine and eternal truth, which is ever present and valid.

When you have found silence and, thereby, have opened up yourself to God, you will slowly open up a road that leads to the truth.

You will experience that as your inner connection grows, your loneliness will decline as you start listening and trusting your inner voice.

From there, a lot of sorrow, anxiety, and loneliness can dissolve, transform into light and love, and fill out the emptiness you feel.

The emptiness is loneliness and anxiety, fear of not being able to find God and, in this, that you are living in shadow and darkness and perceive it to be real.

Darkness is vanity, only there to hold human beings down and prevent them from finding their true nature and relationship to God.

The source of humankind lies with God, and when you recognize this—your true nature—you will let go of fear and anxiety and surrender to the power of light.

Your original reality is in close contact with the divine light, where nothing can scare you because you know that God is ever present at your side.

Rest assured that loneliness can be transformed into energy and vitality as you enhance your trust in God and dare to say, "God, your *will* come true."

Working Sentences for "Feeling Lonely"

- Many people suffer from loneliness.
- Even in the company of others, you may feel lonely.
- The way out of this is through God.
- God is in the silence; the love of God is your life-nerve.
- Your inner connection will slowly remove your sense of loneliness.
- Anxiety lies in the chest as an emptiness. When you realize your connection to God, this void will fill up with light.

26

Self-Discipline

Obtaining self-discipline is one of the most difficult tasks for human beings.

The human mind plays a large role in life and directs every action.

If you, from the bottom of a humble heart, seek self-discipline, you must first learn the literal meaning of the word.

You may think that self-discipline is related to a certain diet, way of life, or habitus, as you struggle to promote this or that ideal way of doing things "right."

Often enough, the discipline that you seek to embody comes from everything other than the self—values that come from others, from surroundings, from society at large.

You suppress your own needs, creating an illusion of discipline by doing or not doing this or that, whatever that may be.

These so-called forms of self-discipline are illusory.

Who else other than God knows your actual self?

Too many people follow the ideas of others on what

their own self consists of and how it should be disciplined. Confusion, vanity, and aimless endeavour follow.

Only God—not books about God or ideas about God but only God—can tell each individual what is right.

To have this guidance directly from its source, we must go into silence and listen to the voice of divine truth within us.

The point that connects the truth of God with the truth of each individual human being is the higher self—hence, self-discipline.

Only the guidance that we receive directly from God by our higher selves, through our hearts, can be labeled a discipline of the self and worthy of following.

When God speaks to the higher self, purification of your heart and cleansing of your karma will be cardinal issues.

In order to cleanse yourself, you—and every human being—must do soul-searching to expose your inner parts, both light and dark, to transform what needs to be transformed in order to be of use to God and humankind alike.

Then you will be asked to guard your actions, your speech, and, not least, your thoughts.

These create energy, and the aim is that this energy should be pure and good and that all that you send out contains the love of God and unselfishness, rather than hurt and egotism.

Thus, your ego will, in time, realize your true desire for purity and universal love and that there is nothing to fear when God shows the ego what is right and wrong.

So be it that everyone must work on self-discipline to his or her own good but in another understanding of the word *self-discipline* than that to which you are wont. You must become a disciple of the self.

Turn your gaze inward, listen to your higher self, and follow the direction given by your higher self in any given situation.

Be mindful, and safely guard everything you send out, be it thought, speech, or action, and know that, in this, you are exercising true discipline of the self.

Self-discipline differs from person to person because each person has his or her own way and his or her own pace. In the end, however, the destination is the same—peace between human beings. And that means love among each other.

To reach this love, to be able to let universal divine love flow freely and effortlessly through you, you must first cleanse yourself in humbleness.

Be grand and look yourself in the eye so that you might see eye to eye with God, which is the epitome of happiness and joy—with peace of mind in the hands of God and with the love of God flowing freely through you.

God blesses your work and follows you dearly, when you are sincere and your heart is pure in your wish for spiritual growth, seeking a closer relationship with God and divine truth.

Working Sentences for "Self-Discipline"

- Many people conceive self-discipline as a certain behavioral mode of being.
- They try to live up to the expectation of themselves from others and society.

- This idea of discipline of the self is illusory, as human beings have derived the framework themselves.
- Only God knows the right framework.
- Through your inner voice, you can connect with divine truth, and when you follow this guidance, you exercise self-discipline.
- Only the guidance that human beings receive from their higher selves can be determined as a self-discipline worthy of following.
- Guard what you send out through thoughts, speech, and actions, and know that this is the true meaning of self-discipline.
- Self-discipline differs from person to person, as we all have our own paths to follow.
- To let love flow freely, you must cleanse yourself in humbleness.
- Look yourself in the eye; then you also will be able to look God in the eye.

27

See Life as a Learning Process

———— —

Dearly beloved human beings:

Perhaps sometimes the road ahead seems narrow and filled with pain.

Know that in these times, when you are most tired and sad, then God is closer to you than ever and supporting and upholding you.

God only wishes that you live in peace and harmony with each other, and the suffering that you experience was never meant to be.

God is always working to uplift you and heighten your energy, but the weight of humanity and your heavy energy takes up a lot of good energy.

It does not mean that this is of no avail but simply that your own attitude toward life could be much lighter and less filled with sorrow.

See your life as a learning process, through which you are made conscious and able to hold and carry the light that earth and all of humanity needs so much.

What you call problems, we call assignments that human beings must solve.

The message of this book—purification and forgiveness—will enable you to rise above the problems and see the bigger perspective: what are you here to learn?

Never doubt the presence of God in your life, and never doubt that God will give you the exact challenge you need in your state of development and your karma in this life.

Whatever you are faced with, you hold the tools and the solutions inside yourself, so turn your gaze inward to find the solution and the way out of the fix you are in.

This is where you lose yourself—when you look to the external world for a way out. The most important thing is to look inward, to find your own truth, and, from there, to act from what you are told.

Make yourself the point of departure for finding your way out of your problems and assignments.

You must seek the cause of the state of affairs in your own inner world, instead of running after others with blame.

It's easy to look at other people with blame, while forgetting your own part.

Dear beloved human beings: look at yourself and know that nothing is pointless. You will see the connection as long as you stay silent and listen to whatever might show in your inner life, as time comes for clarifying your consciousness.

Know that you are beloved and that you can find comfort and encouragement by turning your gaze inward and connecting yourself to God, thereby finding support and love to walk the path you have chosen.

28

Humanity and the Development of the Individual

Dearly beloved human beings:

We encourage you to delve into the message of this book. Try to see yourself in relation to the work that God is doing for humanity and the work that God is doing in you and through you.

It is important that everyone understands their connection to the whole of humanity—that all human beings see themselves as a piece of the puzzle, important to place in order to complete the beautiful picture that God is composing in the light of truth.

All human beings have a free will and a choice of their own. They can set out for the holy grail, or they can take all the detours necessary to see the light of truth.

In the end, the will of God will be fulfilled, and all karma will be resolved. It is up to each human being to shorten or to make longer the way of his or her individual path through his or her own choices.

The sooner you recognize the divine truth of the law of karma, the sooner you will become conscious and can partake in your own wheel of life and influence the karmic incidents in your life, while acknowledging the power of the light of God and the path of your spirit and higher self as your coworker in the many tasks of life.

When you surrender and recognize your humbleness in relation to the divine power, and you ask God to use this force—this light—as an active part of your life, you will experience a more truthful and safer connection that you felt before.

When you reach this stage—where you can stop worrying because you have witnessed, to the last detail, that God has prepared exactly the challenges and opportunity that every human being needs to develop fully—you will realize that all the cards have been dealt by God. The only thing missing is that you start to follow the direction and the advice given to you without hesitation or worry about the outcome.

If the will of God comes true, then you must surrender to this and follow the path, long prepared for humanity and each human being to walk.

Then your footsteps will be blessed, and you will walk this earth in beauty.

Rejoice! You will find a much deeper happiness than you have ever dreamed of and with a whole new level of consciousness.

Take this to your heart: from the spiritual plane, we follow you closely and send all the love and compassion, blessing, and support for you to walk the path of light, to carry the light forward, and to join God's light and divine love.

Through many generations, we have waited for humanity to step into the next phase of development and collective karma.

To resolve and develop your collective karma, you must all take your inner life as point of departure.

From here, all movement starts to obtain the clear and positive vibration that will help humanity and Mother Earth to new healing. In this, all human beings must cleanse and purify themselves in order to let the spirit work directly through them.

As we have described, each one must search his or her soul to find the cornerstone of his or her nature because only by living according to your own nature will you be able to join the vast divine work that lies ahead.

More and more of you will experience that you can take an active part in your own life, inside the framework provided by God.

You are learning to take full responsibility for your life and your actions.

You can never blame others for what happens to you. You must take responsibility yourself, recognizing the law of karma, of cause-and-effect, and give yourself the opportunity and ability to understand what is happening in your life, and thereby see the thin red line of your life thread.

This will help the seekers among you. The

understanding of challenges and life occurrences will be made clear to you so that you can proceeded accordingly to the law of karma, the will of God, and the plan for each individual.

You must understand that you never are to compare yourself with others.

This is the largest mistake—a pitfall for you—yet you spend so much energy on this.

No two human beings are the same or alike; each soul and each individual is unique and precious to God.

Never compare your skills, your ability, or your talents with others because in this, you fail yourself, and you fail God by failing yourself.

God wants you to *see* your own uniqueness and the uniqueness of each individual, as created by the light and love of God. In this, no competition or comparison is possible. This connection is made possible only by the nearness of God to each person.

Comparison only gives you insecurity—enormous and unnecessary in relation to who you really are and your connection to God's wisdom and truth.

Comparison is made up by human beings to induce the use of power, so that the many can be led by the few. As the truth becomes unveiled for your eyes, the only power able to control your life will be the power of God, giving you advice and sharing divine truth and wisdom with each individual.

The purpose lies in your taking control of your life and becoming an instrument of divine love so that you can participate in the healing and restoration of balance of Mother Earth—the collective balance and the positive development of humanity.

Have courage, dear human beings. Know that we are only setting these words on this page to enable you to regain hope, to guide you, and to make you understand the value of each human being and the need for each of you to balance heaven and earth; for everyone, regardless of color or creed, to embrace God and walk safely on the path of the light-bearer, assured that the ultimate truth lies ahead.

No one must think himself or herself unworthy of this. Humankind does not see the worth of itself and does not realize that, to God, all are equally worthy. Difference of class and worthiness is not part of the divine rule, and each of you is, consciously or unconsciously, working toward your own end, decided by you and God.

The only difference is that conscious human beings can help others, partake in the work of purification, and thereby fulfill the plan of God for the benefit of humankind.

Do not ever think that you have the ability to discern or decide who is doing the work of God, as God has mysterious ways. What seems hopeless or abandoned may carry a deep and magnificent meaning.

Rest assured that according to the will of God, nothing is wasted or in vain, as everything, even the smallest incident or episode, gives you an experience that is needed to become full-blown carriers of the light of God.

Working Sentences for "Humanity and the Development of the Individual"

- See yourself in the connection between God's work for humanity and God's work for you.
- Recognize your connection to humanity.
- See yourself as part of a whole.
- All human beings have a free will and a free choice.
- Realize God is your coworker and helper in this life.
- Learn to understand the red line running through your life.
- *Do not ever compare yourself with others.*
- No two human beings are alike. You are unique.
- God wants you to see this uniqueness as a reflection of God´s love and light.
- You must take an active part in healing the balance of earth and the collective development of humanity.
- Each one is needed to create this balance.
- When you surrender, true comfort will follow.
- You will stop worrying.
- Your journey will depart from your own inner life, and all action must come from a purified heart.
- Find the cornerstone of your nature to life, accordingly.
- Learn to take full responsibility for your life and actions.
- The conscious human being can draw others into the work of purification.

29

Self-Realization

———

Dear humanity:

When you talk of realizing yourself, you most often refer to your own personality.

You must develop yourself and become more conscious, and many millions across the world are working on this.

You are working on the mind, emotions, and thoughts—meaning, the intellect.

You must mature and grow your own experience during the walk of life.

Many people realize that this development of the self has a natural continuation.

This continuation is called development of the self on a spiritual plane.

You must realize your higher self, which is the true meaning of any self-realization.

You are working to become spiritually conscious, and you reconnect to your higher self through your heart.

Your higher self has been denied contact from you because you have shut down your heart and have not maintained your heart connection with yourself, the higher truth, and the divine truth. In this way, you have lost your sense of God and the divine wisdom, and you live your life as a boat without a rudder.

"My life to live," you may say, and yes, you are right, but life is also about understanding and making experiences through reflecting on your actions, in order to create positive karma for yourself and humankind—and for Mother Earth, as your karma has been woven together.

You must realize that balance can be obtained only if each individual takes responsibility for his or her life, actions, relationships, and karma, so that these human beings may work in unison, thereby drawing all of humanity into a positive development, where heart and spirit will reign, and humankind will realize that it must work together with God to heal the planet.

This cooperation must stem from a humble wish to cleanse yourself and to live according to the plan of God for each individual. As more and more realize this, the development toward healing humanity and Mother Earth will accelerate.

Light wants to come down on earth, and your test will be to carry this light, which is already placed in your heart, as the biggest cleansing and healing power there is.

By opening up your heart, you will make contact with your spirit through your higher self, and you will realize that the contact with God has always been there and will always be there, except when you have shut down this natural connection.

God will rejoice when the many find their way back to this connection. As your heart opens, hope and light will be brought from you to others around you who are still trying to find their way through night and fog.

Know that you are a light-bearer and divine servant, and your servitude is to emanate and live the love of God on all planes, while taking part in earthly life, thereby manifesting that heaven can be brought to earth by the spirit that you incarnate.

May God be with you and bless you in your
work for light, earth, and humanity.
—The White Brotherhood

Working Sentences for "Self-Realization"

- Many people are involved in self-realization.
- Self-realization has a higher meaning; namely, the realization of the higher self.
- You must realize your higher self, your spirit.
- This is true realization of the self.
- Life must be understood and made into experience.
- All human beings must be responsible for themselves and their karma.
- Mother Earth and humankind are interdependent.
- Healing Mother Earth must take place in cooperation between spirit and humans.

- God will rejoice when the many seek connection to the divine and will work through your heart to send light into darkness.
- Bearers of the light serve God by emanating love and wisdom through an active earthly life.
- Heaven can be brought down on earth by the power of your spirit.

Translator's Note

In this text, the word *God* appears a number of times, mostly in the context of a name that could point to the male God, Jehovah or Yahve, known from the Old Testament, as well as to the Lord Jesus Christ.

Of these miscellaneous interpretations, the White Brotherhood writes in chapter 6, "We suggest that you call upon any deity or guardian that is especially helpful and benevolent to you. It could be God, Christ, the Holy Mother, or anyone who feels right for you when you are working with forgiveness. *In this book, we have chosen God.*" This terminology points both to the openness of using God as a concept developed by different religions and the specific monotheistic God of Judaism, Islam, and the Christian Trinity.

In this translation, the difference between the concept of God and the name of God (meaning Yahve) has been resolved by using the word God (as concept) and refraining from using gender-specific pronouns.

In this, I have based myself on the following statement from chapter 22: "God has no form but will always be present in the shape of light, the light of divine love." If, for the sake of understanding, I was forced to be gender specific (i.e., "her image," chapter 20), I have done so according to the belief that "all things are borne of woman."

Printed in the United States
by Baker & Taylor Publisher Services